Talk About the Cover

Puppies

Puppies, puppies, please sit still.

This **BIG** dog is not a hill.

Climb a ladder or a TREE.

Please, please, please don't
climb on **ME**!

How high can YOU climb?

ISBN 0-15-334283-8

2 3 4 5 6 7 8 9 10   048   10 09 08 07 06 05 04

Authors

Alma Flor Ada • F. Isabel Campoy • Yolanda N. Padrón • Nancy Roser

Harcourt

Orlando   Austin   Chicago   New York   Toronto   London   San Diego

Visit *The Learning Site!*
www.harcourtschool.com

UNIT
1
SELF-DISCOVERY

CONTENTS

Self-Discovery

Review Vocabulary with a Play
★ STORIES ON STAGE ★

CONTENTS

UNIT **2** WORKING TOGETHER

Working Together

Review Vocabulary with a Play
STORIES ON STAGE

CONTENTS

UNIT **3** GROWTH AND CHANGE

Growth and Change

Review Vocabulary with a Play
★ STORIES ON STAGE ★

4

CONTENTS

Creativity

Review Vocabulary with a Play
STORIES ON STAGE

CONTENTS

Communities

Review Vocabulary with a Play
STORIES ON STAGE

CONTENTS

Explorations

Review Vocabulary with a Play

STORIES ON STAGE

Use What You Know

■ When You Read and Write

I don't know what **glad** means.

I think about my birthday.

I think **glad** means **happy**.

■ When You Listen and Speak

I have a dog at home.

I know what Miss Kim is talking about.

I can tell people about dogs.

Find Help

■ When You Read and Write

- I can look in a **dictionary**.
- I can ask a **friend**.
- I can ask my **teacher**.

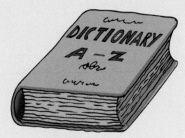

dictionary

friend

teacher

What does wild mean?

■ When You Listen and Speak

- I can raise my hand.
- I can ask a question.
- I can write a question.

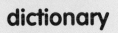

9

Make Connections

■ When You Read and Write

I go to the park.

I read a book about a park.

I can write about the park.

I see ducks at the park.

■ When You Listen and Speak

This is a cub.

I see a baby bear.

I hear Mrs. Jones say **cub**.

I think a **cub** is a baby bear.

Picture It

■ When You Read and Listen

I make a picture in my mind.

It helps me understand what I read.

It helps me understand what I hear.

■ When You Write and Speak

I make a picture in my mind.

I can write about the picture.

I can talk about the picture.

Look for Patterns

■ When You Read and Listen

What does **violet** mean?

I know that blue is a color.

I know that green is a color.

Violet must be a color, too!

This hat is **blue**.   This hat is **green**.   This hat is **violet**.

■ When You Listen and Speak

The dog is big.

The horse is bigger.

I hear a pattern!

Bigger sounds like **big**.

Set a Purpose

■ When You Read and Listen

I can ask myself

- What am I reading?
- Who is talking?
- What do I want to know?

■ When You Write and Speak

I can ask myself

- Who will read this?
- Who is listening?
- What do I want to say?

13

14

I'm Happy to Be Me!

I'm happy to be me!

I'm happy to be me!

As I grow, I'll always know,

I'm happy to be me!

*Sing to the tune of
"The Farmer in the Dell."*

Make Predictions

Look at the picture. Think about
what will happen next.

This picture shows what will happen
next. She will kick the ball.

Try This

▶ Look at the picture. Think about what will happen next.

What will happen next?

- The boy will ride his bike.

- The boy will read a book.

Vocabulary POWER

My Day at School ▼

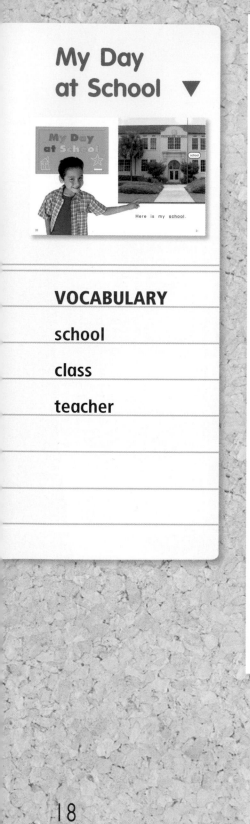

VOCABULARY

school

class

teacher

Children go to **school**.

A **teacher** helps you learn.

We take turns in my **class**.

school

Here is my school.

Here is my class.

teacher

Here is my teacher.

Here is my friend.

Here I am.

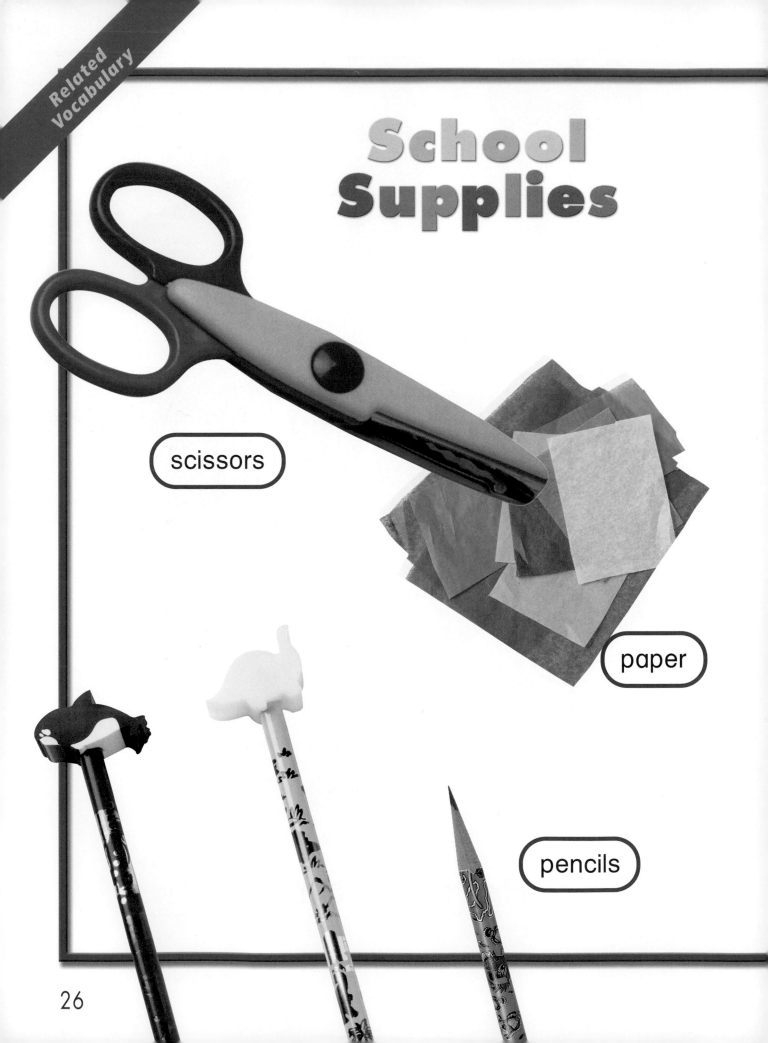

School Supplies

scissors

paper

pencils

crayons

books

Think Critically

① Who does the boy see at school?

② What did the boy paint?

③ How is this school like your school?

④ What do you like about your school?

Vocabulary POWER

Families ▼

Families do many things together.

VOCABULARY

families

help

eat

talk

laugh

Families **help** each other.

It is time to **eat**.

Families **talk** with each other.

We **laugh** at funny things.

Families

Families like to help.

Families like to eat.

Families like to talk.

Families like to play.

Families like to laugh, too.

Think Critically

❶ What do families like to do?

❷ How do families play together?

❸ How can you tell these families like to be together?

❹ What did you like best about this story?

Clap Your Hands ▼

VOCABULARY

knees

nose

chin

toes

arms

eyes

hands

They wear pads on their **knees**.

She is touching her **nose**.

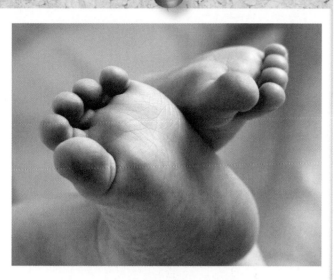

A baby has little **toes**.

His hand is on his **chin**.

They use their **hands** and **arms** to hold books.

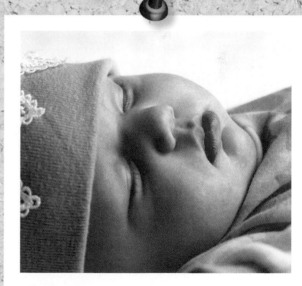

The baby closes her **eyes**.

Pat your knees.

Pat your nose.

Pat your chin.

40

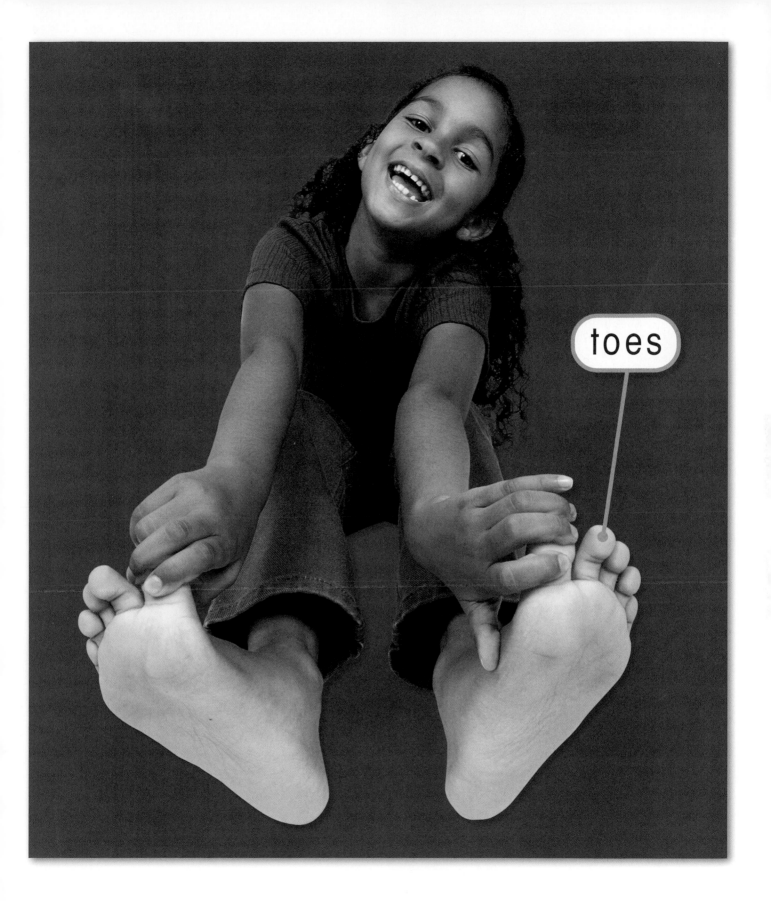

toes

Pat your toes.

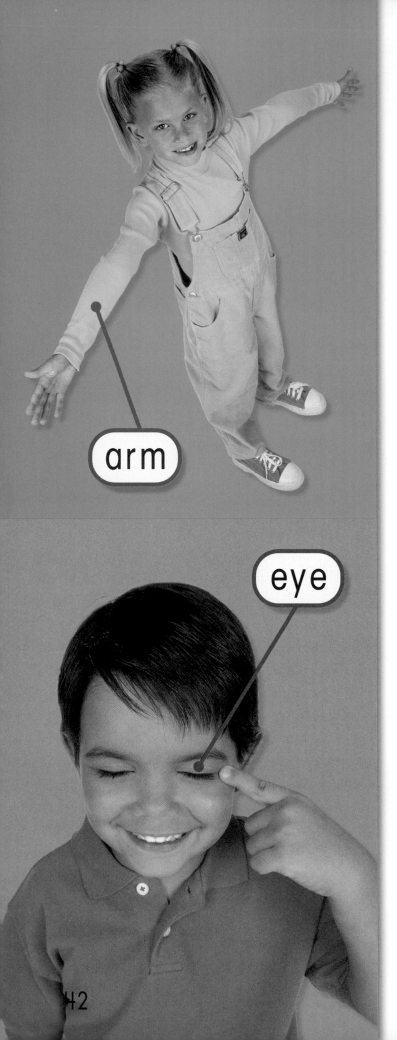

arm

eye

42

Open your arms.

Close your eyes.

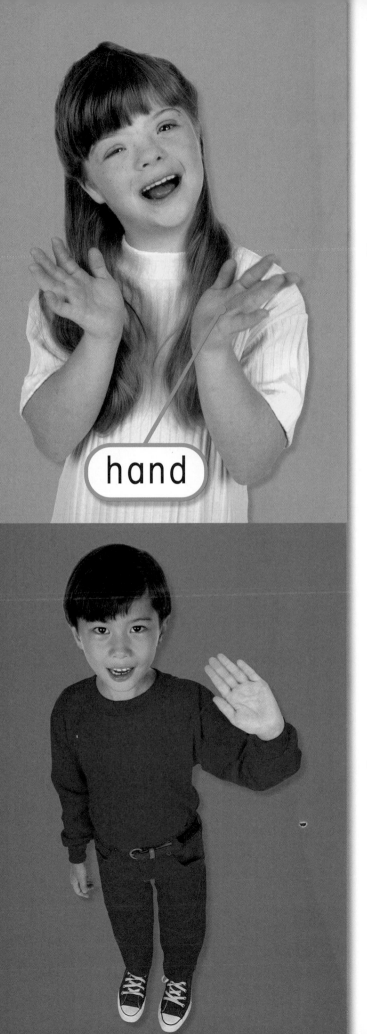

hand

Clap your hands.

Wave good-bye!

43

My Body

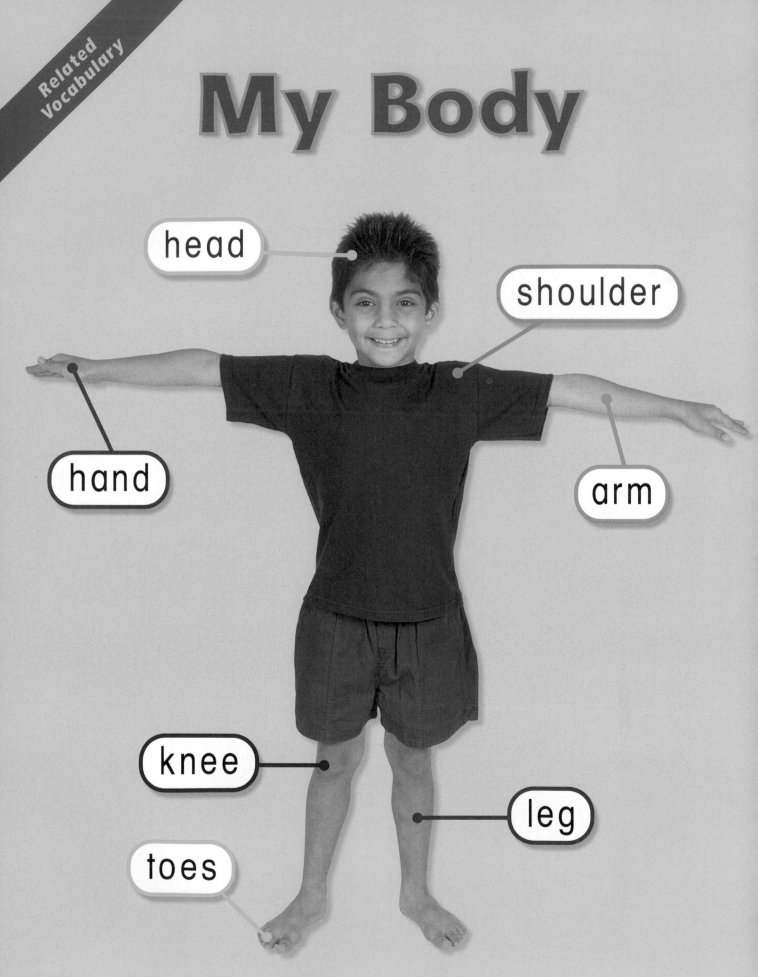

head

shoulder

hand

arm

knee

leg

toes

44

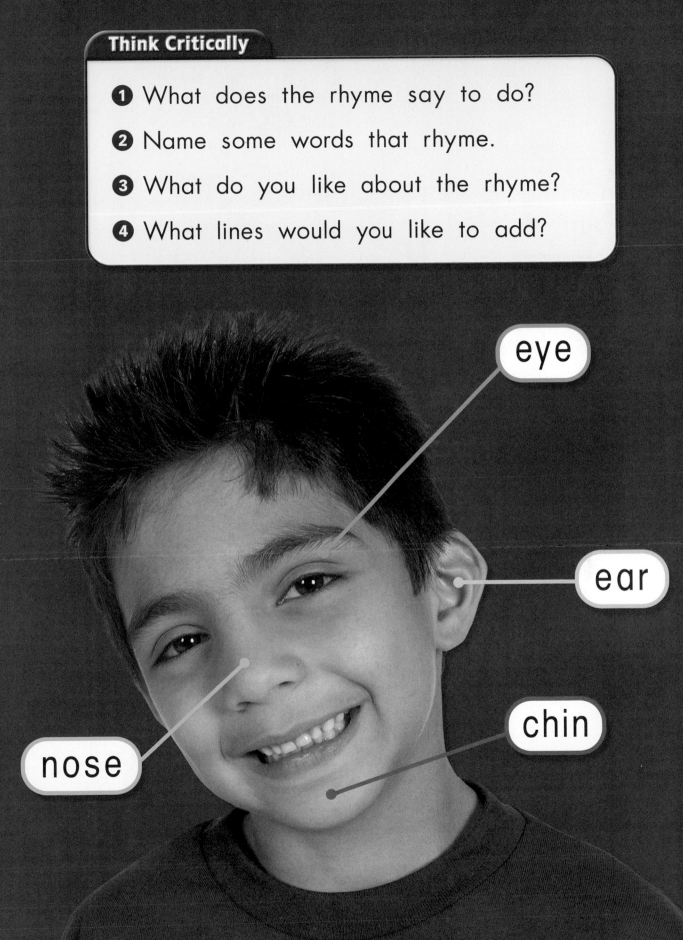

Think Critically

❶ What does the rhyme say to do?

❷ Name some words that rhyme.

❸ What do you like about the rhyme?

❹ What lines would you like to add?

eye

ear

chin

nose

45

Vocabulary POWER

Down on the Farm ▼

VOCABULARY

nap

swim

ride

farm

The child is taking a **nap**.

I like to **swim** in the pool.

I can **ride** my bike.

Cows live on this **farm**.

Down on

by
Rita
Lascaro

the Farm

I see my dog play.

I can play like my dog.

I see my cat nap.

I can nap like my cat.

I see my hen flap.

I can flap like my hen.

I see my duck swim.

I can swim like my duck.

I see my friends ride.

I can ride like my friends...

...down on the farm.

❶ What things can the girl do?

❷ Do you think she feels proud? Why or why not?

❸ What are some things you can do?

❹ What did you like best about this story?

61

Review Vocabulary with a Play

★ STORIES ON STAGE ★

Look at Us!

Review

VOCABULARY

school

help

class

hands

ride

nap

Characters

Red Birds

Blue Birds

Blue Bears

Red Bears

 Look at us!

 We go to school.

 Look at us!

 We help the class.

 Look at us!

 We can play.

 Look at us!

 We clap our hands.

67

 Look at us!

 We ride our bikes.

Look at us!

 We can nap!
Good night!

Review Activities

Think and Respond

1. **Name two places where children spend a lot of time.**

2. **Which two stories tell about these places? What do they say?**

3. **Which stories tell about things children can do? What do they say?**

4. **What is the same about the stories?**

5. **Which story is your favorite?**

VOCABULARY REVIEW

All About Me Circle

Trace a circle and cut it out.
Draw yourself in the middle.
Write Vocabulary words that tell about you.

Make Introductions

Make a stick puppet of yourself. Let your puppet meet your classmates' puppets. Take turns making your puppets say these sentences.

Hello. My name is _____.

What is your name?

We Will Work Together

You help me
And I'll help you
And we will work together.
We can be a team!
We can be a team!
We can be a team!
Yes, we will work together.

Sing to the tune of "Bingo."

PEAS

SEEDS

Setting

The setting of a story is the place where the story happens. Look at the picture. What is the setting?

The setting is a classroom. How did you know?

Try This

▶ Look at the pictures. Choose the word that names the setting of each picture. Then tell how you know.

Which word names the setting?

- park
- farm
- bedroom

Which word names the setting?

- school
- zoo
- backyard

Vocabulary POWER

Our Team ▼

We are a team.

VOCABULARY

team

listen

win

lose

fun

It is **fun** to play games.

Our **team** is happy when we **win**.

We feel sad if we **lose**.

I like to **listen** to stories.

We are a team.

We listen.

We take turns.

We help each other.

Some days we win.

Some days we lose.

We always have fun.
We are a team!

Baseball

helmet

bat

field

1. What does this team do?

2. Why do people on teams need to listen?

3. Why do people on teams take turns?

4. What is fun about being on a team?

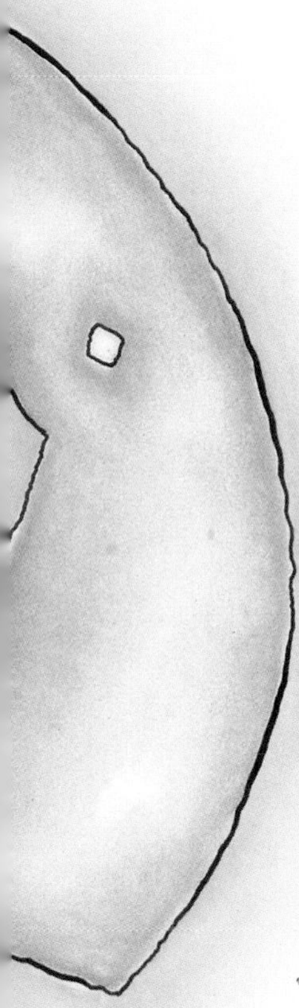

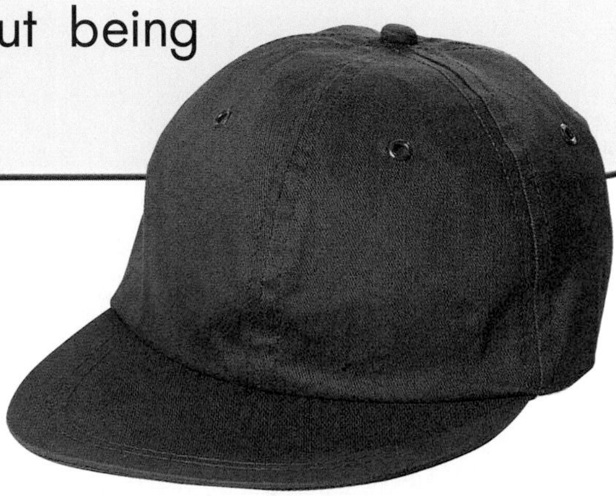

glove

cap

ball

87

Vocabulary POWER

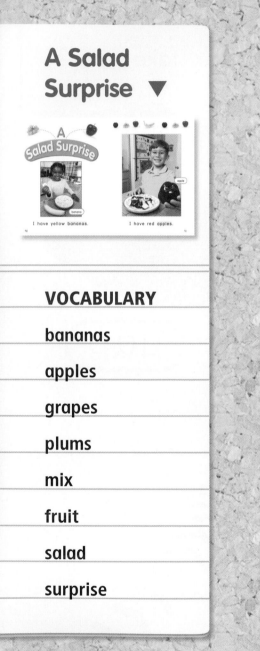

A Salad Surprise ▼

I have yellow bananas.

I have red apples.

VOCABULARY

bananas

apples

grapes

plums

mix

fruit

salad

surprise

There are many ways to make a **salad**.

Can you find **bananas** and **plums** in the picture?

Apples and **grapes** are good to eat.

A **surprise** can be fun.

The girls **mix** the batter in a bowl.

There are many different kinds of **fruit** .

A Salad Surprise

banana

I have yellow bananas.

apple

I have red apples.

grapes

I have green grapes.

plum

I have purple plums.

fruit salad

We mix all the fruit.
Now we have fruit salad.

Surprise!

Think Critically

❶ What do the children make?

❷ How do they all work together?

❸ Do you think the boy is surprised?

❹ What would you put in your own fruit salad?

Vocabulary POWER

Animal Friends ▼

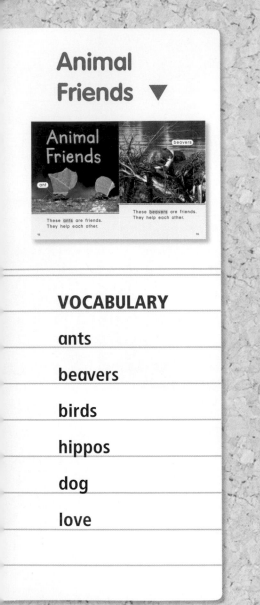

VOCABULARY

ants

beavers

birds

hippos

dog

love

The **ants** are on a leaf.

Beavers have flat tails.

Hippos have big mouths.

Birds have feathers.

The dog has a black nose.

I love my mom.

Animal Friends

ant

These **ants** are friends.
They help each other.

beavers

These beavers are friends.
They help each other.

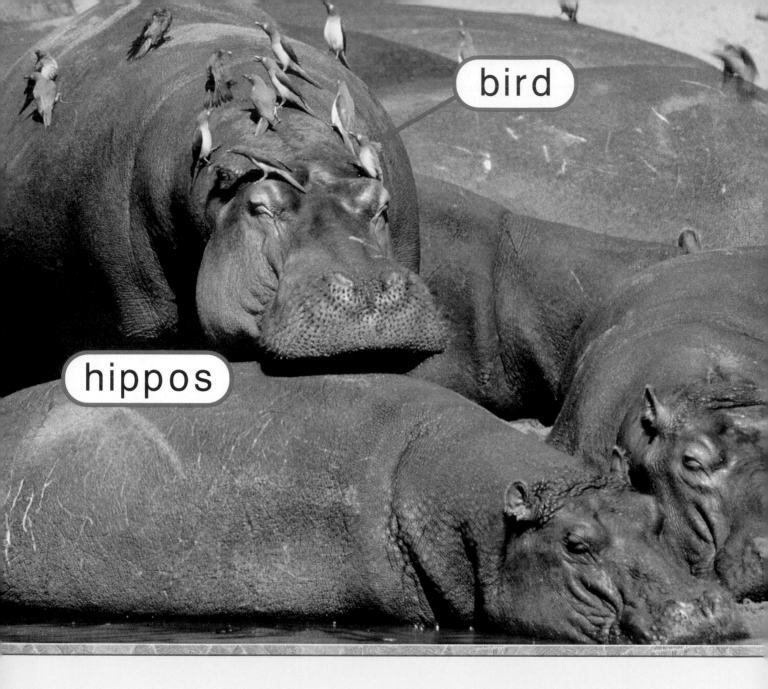

bird

hippos

The birds and the hippos are friends. They help each other.

dog

person

The dog and the person are friends. They help each other. They love each other, too!

Think Critically

❶ How do the animals help each other?

❷ Name some other animals that help each other.

❸ How do you help your friends?

❹ What surprised you about this story?

Vocabulary POWER

The Big, Big Wall ▼

VOCABULARY

wall

fall

two

three

together

smiled

down

The children sit on a **wall**.

The boy has **two** red shoes.

The girls **smiled** for their picture.

The **three** friends work **together**.

The girl is sliding **down**.

The leaves **fall** from the tree.

The Big, Big Wall

by Reginald Howard

illustrated by Jose Aruego and Ariane Dewey

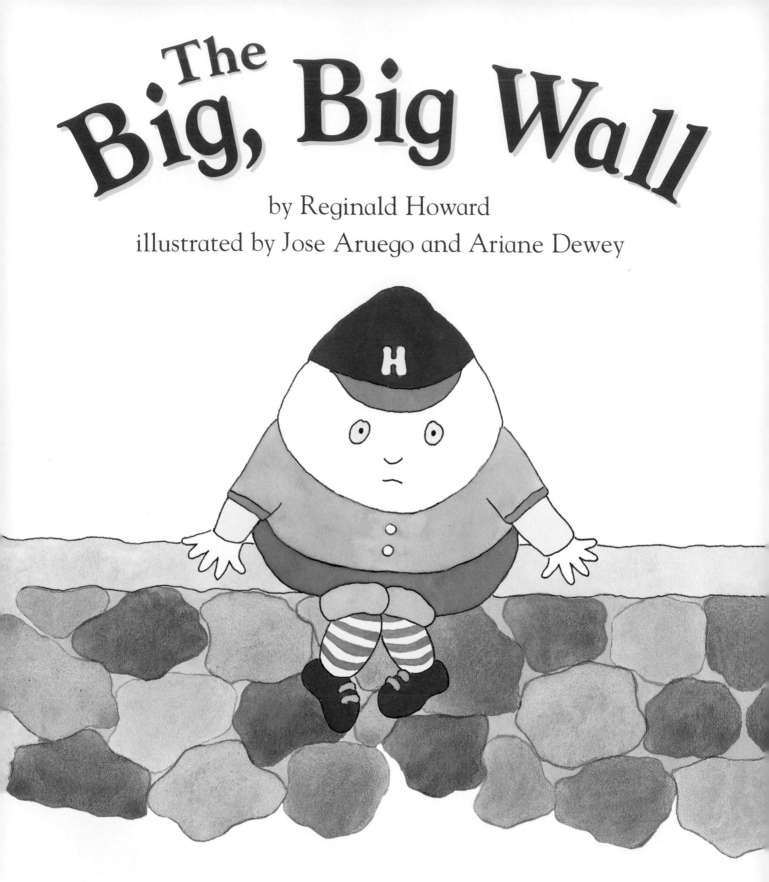

Humpty Dumpty sat on a wall.

He did not want to
have a big fall.

One friend came to
the big, big wall.

"I will help you. You
will not fall."

Two friends came to
the big, big wall.

"We will help you. You
will not fall."

Three friends came to
the big, big wall.

"We will all come together.
You will not fall."

Humpty Dumpty smiled
at his friends.

"Now I will come back down again."

Think Critically

1 How did Humpty feel before his friends came?

2 Why do you think Humpty Dumpty was afraid?

3 How did Humpty Dumpty's friends help him?

4 What did you like best about this story?

113

Review Vocabulary with a Play

★ STORIES ON STAGE ★

The Grasshoppers and the Ants

Review

VOCABULARY

together

grapes

fun

apples

ants

Characters

Busy Ants

Worker Ants

Gus Grasshopper

Gail Grasshopper

 We are working together.

 We are getting some
big grapes.

 We are not working.

 We are having fun.

 We are working together.

 We are getting some apples.

 We are not working.

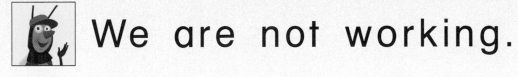 We are playing with our friend.

 Winter is here.

 We worked together!

 We did not work.

 The ants were right!
Next time we will work!

Review Activities

Think and Respond

1. What is the same about the stories?

2. How are the characters helpers?

3. Pick two characters. How are they alike?

4. Which stories were funny? Why?

5. Which stories did you like best? Why?

Building Sentences

Get four cards. Write an animal word on the first card. Write <u>eat</u> on the second card. Write a food word on the third card. Write a period on the fourth card. Build and read sentences. Trade cards with classmates.

Ants eat grapes .

122

LANGUAGE STRUCTURE REVIEW

Describe Surroundings

Draw a face with eyes, ears, and a nose.
Find a partner. Then do these things:

1. Think of a place.

2. Point to the eyes and tell what you see.

3. Point to the ears and tell what you hear.

4. Point to the nose and tell what you smell.

5. Ask your partner to guess the place.

SING ALONG

We Are Growing

We are growing every day,
Every day,
Every day.
We are growing every day
And soon we will be big!

*Sing to the tune of
"Mary Had a Little Lamb"*

Sequence

In a story, things happen in an order that makes sense.

Look at these pictures. What happens first, next, and last?

First

Next

Last

Try This

▶ Look at these pictures. They are not in the right order. Think about what happens first, next, and last.

What happens first, next, and last?

What happens first, next, and last?

Vocabulary POWER

Now I Can ▼

VOCABULARY

kick

soccer

paint

flowers

read

books

The girl can **kick** the ball.

It takes practice to play **soccer** well.

128

I like to **paint**.

The field is full of **flowers**.

We like to **read books**.

Now I Can

by **Margaret Matthews**

photography by **Shelley Rotner**

soccer ball

When I was little,
I couldn't kick.

Now I can kick.
I can play soccer.

paint

When I was little,
I couldn't paint well.

paintbrush

Now I can paint very well.
I can paint flowers.

book

When I was little,
I couldn't read.

Now I can read.
I can read lots of books.

We can do lots of
things now.

What can you do?

Growing Up

4 years old

2 years old

6 months old

138

8 years old

6 years old

Think Critically

❶ What did the children learn to do?

❷ How do you think they learned these things?

❸ What else do children learn to do?

❹ How do you feel when you learn new things?

Vocabulary POWER

Dan's Pet ▼

VOCABULARY

baby

chick

pet

eggs

The **chick** is fluffy.

The **baby** is smiling.

A dog is a good **pet** to have.

The **eggs** are in a nest.

Dan's Pet

by Alma Flor Ada
illustrated by Brian Karas

Dan held a small baby chick.

"Can I have her as a pet?"
"Yes, Dan," said Mama.

"I'll call her Jen," said Dan.

Dan helped with Jen.

Dan fed Jen every day.

Jen got very big!

One day, Dan didn't see Jen.
"Jen! Jen!" called Dan.

"Jen is in here," said Mama.
"Look at her eggs."

"Oh my!" said Dan.
"Now I will have lots of pets!"

Think Critically

1 What does Dan's pet do?

2 Is Dan surprised? How do you know?

3 Could this story really happen?

4 Would you like to have pets like Dan's? Why or why not?

Vocabulary POWER

Good-bye and Hello ▼

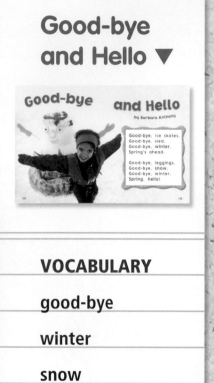

VOCABULARY

good-bye

winter

snow

spring

hello

I kiss my mother **good-bye**.

Their friends came to say **hello**.

We ride our sled in **winter**.

Flowers bloom in **spring**.

Everything is covered
with **snow**.

Good-bye

and Hello

by Barbara Anthony

Good-bye, ice skates.
Good-bye, sled.
Good-bye, winter.
Spring's ahead.

Good-bye, leggings.
Good-bye, snow.
Good-bye, winter.
Spring, hello!

Hello, crocus.
Hello, kite.
Good-bye, winter.
Spring's in sight.

Hello, jump rope.
Hello, swing.
Good-bye winter!
Hello, spring!

Weather Words

sunny

rainy

snowy

windy

foggy

Think Critically

❶ What might you see in the spring?

❷ What might you see in the winter?

❸ What are the other two seasons?

❹ Which season do you like the best?

Vocabulary POWER

Seeds Grow ▼

VOCABULARY

plant

seeds

ground

roots

leaves

sun

rain

air

I can **plant** the **seeds** in the soil.

The tree's **roots** are under the **ground**.

This new plant has small **leaves**.

The **air** is filled with **rain**.

The **sun** is bright.

Seeds Grow

by Angela Shelf Medearis

illustrated by Jill Dubin

We plant some seeds in the ground.

We sprinkle
water all around.

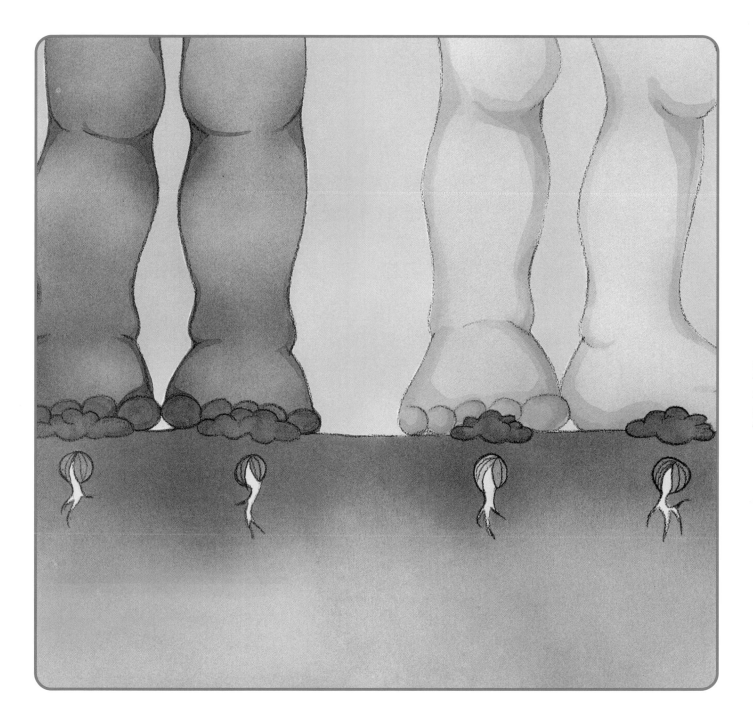

Soon roots push out . . .

. . . and then
down, down, down.

Little shoots
now come out.

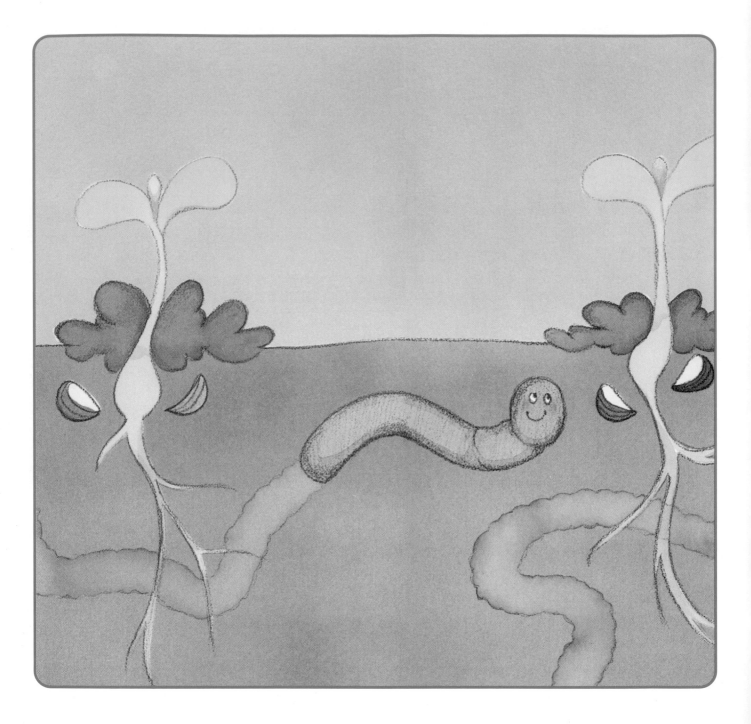

Then the shoots
start to sprout.

The leaves unfold,
one by one.

The buds grow up
toward the sun.

The petals unfold
and turn to gold.

Rain showers water the flowers.

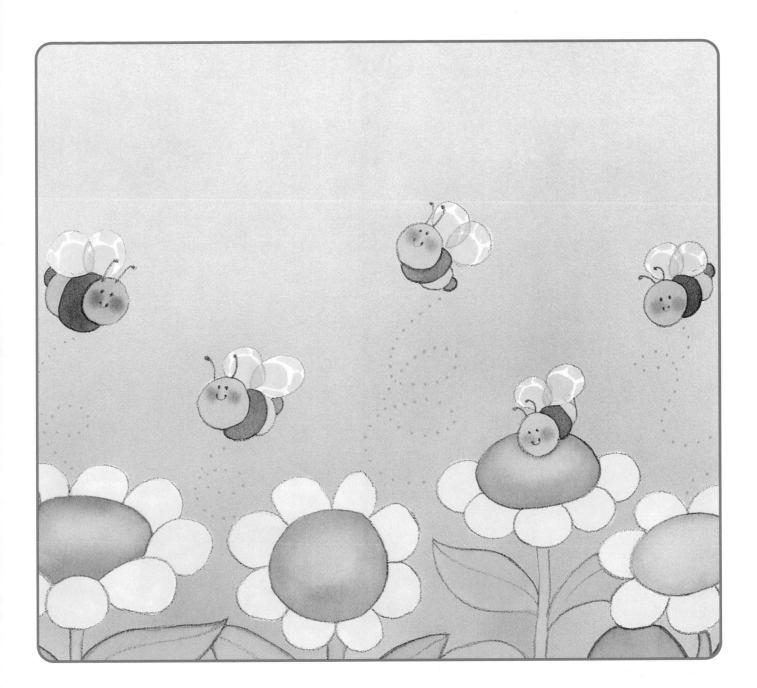

Bees buzz here and there.

Sweet smells fill the air. Pretty sunflowers are everywhere.

Think Critically

1 What did the children first do to the seeds?

2 What happened to the seeds next?

3 What kind of flowers grew from the seeds?

4 What plants have you seen grow?

Everything Changes

176

Characters

Mrs. Chen

Marco

Emma

Devon

Clara

Don

children

Look at all the things that change!

 We plant seeds. Then the seeds grow into flowers.

 Everything changes!

 The sun comes up.
The sun goes down.

 Everything changes!

 Eggs are in a nest.
Soon baby birds will
come out!

Everything changes!

It was winter.
Now it's spring!

Everything changes!

I'm a boy. Now I'm a rabbit.

Let's all be rabbits!

Come on, rabbits.
It's time to eat!

Review Activities

Think and Respond

1 What changes in "Now I Can"?

2 What changes in "Good-bye and Hello"?

3 How are all the stories alike?

4 Which characters made you laugh? Why?

5 Which story had the best ending? Why?

VOCABULARY REVIEW

Word Flap Book

Fold a sheet of paper in half. Cut three flaps. Write a Vocabulary word on each flap. Draw a matching picture under the flap.

LANGUAGE STRUCTURE REVIEW

Express Likes and Dislikes

Draw two things you like. Next, draw two things you don't like. Put your paper on the floor. Toss a marker. If the marker lands on something you like, say

I like _____.

If the marker lands on something you don't like, say

I don't like _____.

UNIT 4 CREATIVITY

SING ALONG

You Can Dream!

Dream of this!
Dream of that!
Dream that you're a great big cat.
When you want to be a tiger at the zoo,
You can dream! That's what to do!

 Sing to the tune of "This Old Man."

Making Inferences

Look at the picture and read the sentence.

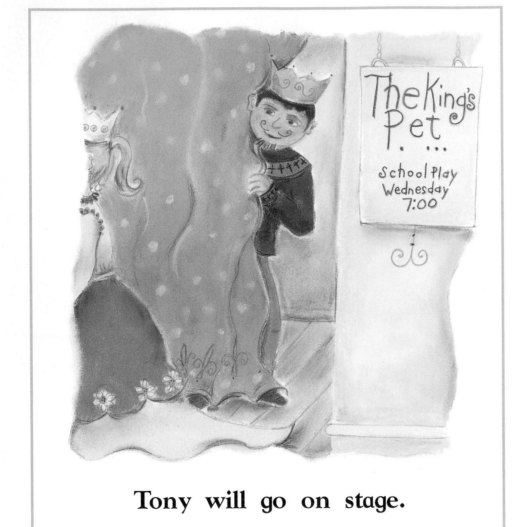

Tony will go on stage.

You know these things about Tony.

- Tony is in a play.

- Tony is a king in the play.

- Tony will go on stage.

Try This

▶ Look at the picture and read the sentence. Which sentences tell about Jill?

Jill loves to paint.

- Jill has two brothers.

- Jill loves to paint.

- Jill likes pizza.

- Jill is going to paint a flower.

Vocabulary POWER

Stretch, Stretch ▼

VOCABULARY

stretch

high

try

sky

fly

pretend

We **stretch** our muscles before we exercise.

The balloons are **high** in the **sky**.

Let's **fly** a kite.

We can **pretend** we are grown up.

He will **try** to ride the bike.

Stretch, Stretch

by Louise Binder Scott

Stretch, stretch
way up high.
Stretch and try
to reach the sky.

193

Be a bird,
fly to a tree.
Be a fish,
swim in the sea.

Sway and sway,
just like a breeze.
Now pretend
you're going to sneeze.

Think Critically

1 What do the animals pretend to be?

2 What would you like to pretend to be?

3 What is one thing in the rhyme that people can do?

4 What part of the rhyme do you like the best?

Vocabulary POWER

When the TV Broke ▼

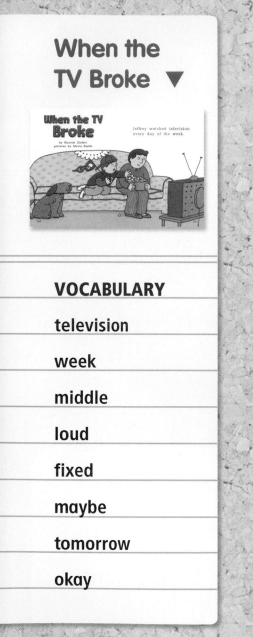

VOCABULARY

television

week

middle

loud

fixed

maybe

tomorrow

okay

A **week** is seven days long.

The boy gave a **loud** shout.

The boy in the **middle** is wearing a white shirt.

The **television** was **fixed**.

Maybe I will be a firefighter when I grow up.

The doctor says the girl will feel **okay tomorrow**.

When the TV Broke

by Harriet Ziefert
pictures by Mavis Smith

Jeffrey watched television every day of the week.

Jeffrey watched on
Monday . . .

on Tuesday . . .

on Wednesday . . .

on Thursday . . .

on Friday . . .

and on Saturday.

On Sunday right in the
middle of a gorilla movie—

the TV made a loud "buzz!"
The picture faded and . . .

the screen went black.

Jeffrey's mom turned
all the dials.
But nothing happened.

On Monday Jeffrey's dad
put the TV into the car.

Jeffrey sat on the sofa.
Now he had nothing to do.

On Tuesday Jeffrey asked,
"Is the TV fixed yet?"

"Not yet," Jeffrey's mom said.
"Maybe tomorrow."

On Wednesday Jeffrey
said, "It's tomorrow.
Is the TV fixed yet?"

"Not yet," she said.
"Maybe tomorrow."

213

On Thursday Jeffrey said,
"It's tomorrow.
Is the TV fixed yet?"

"Not yet," Mom said.
"Maybe tomorrow."

"What are you doing?"
asked Jeffrey's sister.
"Nothing much," he said.

"Will you read to me?"
she asked.
"Okay," said Jeffrey.

Then it was Friday.

Jeffrey found some boxes.

He found paint . . .
scissors . . . crayons . . .
and glue, too.

"What are you doing?"
asked Jeffrey's sister.

"Nothing much," he said.

"What are you doing now?"
asked Jeffrey's sister.

"Nothing much," he said.

On Saturday Dad
called, "I'm home!
Come and watch TV.
It's all fixed!"

"Not now, Dad," said Jeffrey.
"I'm busy. Maybe tomorrow."

Think Critically

1. What does Jeffrey do after the TV breaks?

2. Is there a pattern to what Jeffrey and his sister say? What is it?

3. Do you think Jeffrey will watch TV as much now?

4. What would you do if your TV broke?

225

Vocabulary POWER

Tools for Artists ▼

VOCABULARY

artist

makes

tools

use

builds

pictures

The **artist** is painting outside.

We **use** **tools** to do many things.

226

A potter **makes** pots from clay.

This man **builds** houses.

The woman will choose one of the **pictures**.

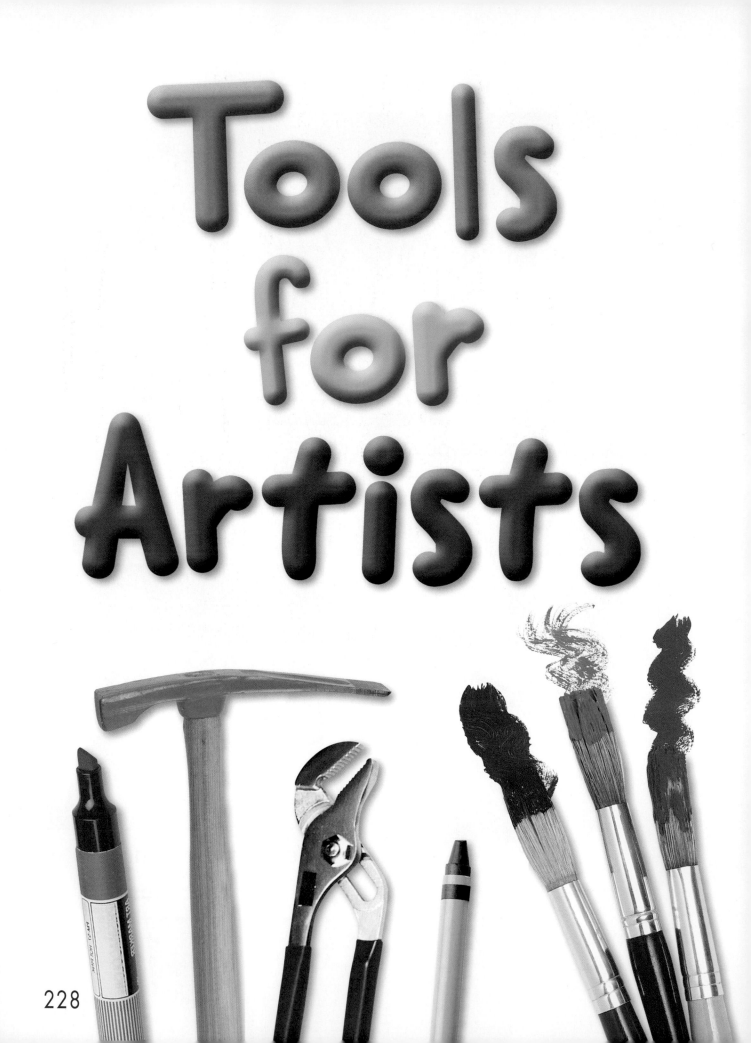

Tools for Artists

This artist makes bowls.
She turns the wheel
around very fast. What
tools does she use?

This artist carves wood.
He is making a wooden bear.
What tools does he use?

This artist builds things
with parts that move.
What tools does he use?

This artist paints pictures.
She is painting a building.
What tools does she use?

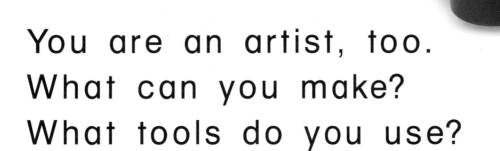

You are an artist, too.
What can you make?
What tools do you use?

Think Critically

❶ What is the same about all the artists?

❷ What tools do artists use?

❸ Why do you think artists make things?

❹ Which tools do you like to use?

Vocabulary POWER

Tomás Rivera ▼

VOCABULARY

born

crops

stories

library

job

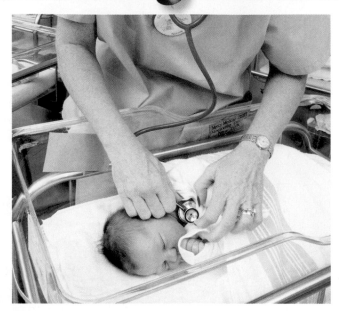

This baby was just **born**.

A teacher has an important **job**.

We can find great **stories** in books.

A **library** has many books.

The **crops** are planted in rows.

Tomás Rivera

by Jane Medina
illustrated by Ed Martinez

Tomás Rivera was born in Texas. Tomás and his family went from farm to farm picking crops.

Tomás helped pick crops all day. It was hard work. At night he had fun with his Grandpa.

"Come quick, children!" Grandpa called. "It's time for stories!"

"You tell the best stories!"
Tomás said. "I want to
tell good stories, too."

"We can get lots of stories for you, Tomás," said Grandpa. "When?" asked Tomás.

"Let's go now!" Grandpa said with a wink. "Quick, hop in!"

"This is a library," said Grandpa. "Look at all the books!" yelled Tomás as he clapped his hands.

"Read all you can, Tomás. It will help you think of lots of stories," said Grandpa.

Tomás started thinking of his own stories. Then he started writing them.

When he grew up, Tomás got a job as a teacher. He still kept writing stories.

His stories tell about picking crops, just as his family did. Lots of people read his books.

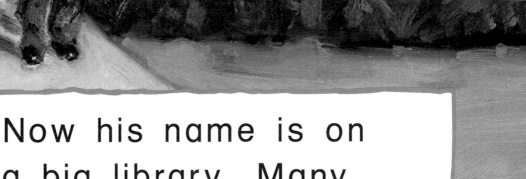

Now his name is on
a big library. Many
people visit the library.
They get books, just
as Tomás did.

Welcome to the Library

globe

shelf

librarian

picture book

computer

chair

table

Think Critically

❶ What did Grandpa do at night for the children?

❷ Why did Tomás want to tell his own stories?

❸ Why do you think Tomás Rivera wrote stories about people picking crops?

❹ What did you like best about this story?

Review Vocabulary with a Play

STORIES ON STAGE ★

Let's Pretend

Review
VOCABULARY
okay
pretend
job
fly
artist
middle

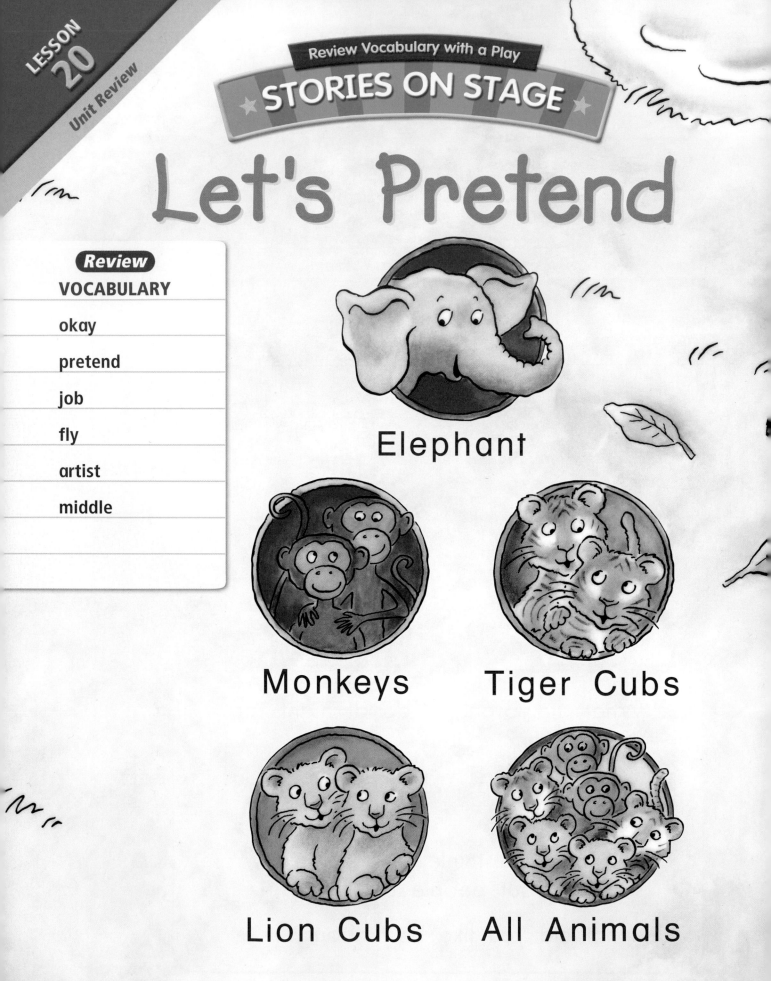

Elephant

Monkeys

Tiger Cubs

Lion Cubs

All Animals

250

 Let's play a game today!

 Okay! Let's play pretend!
Your job is leader.

 Pretend you're a bird.
Flap your wings!

 Flap! Flap! Fly!

252

 Pretend you're an artist. Show me your brushes!

 Dip! Brush! Brush!

253

 Pretend you're a frog. Jump into the middle of the pond!

 Hop! Hop! Splash!

 Pretend you're an animal.

 We don't have to pretend we're animals! We ARE animals, Elephant!

255

Review Activities

Think and Respond

1 Jeffrey has some good ideas. What other characters have good ideas?

2 How is Jeffrey like Tomás Rivera?

3 How is "Stretch, Stretch" like "Let's Pretend"?

4 Which character is most like you? Why?

5 Which story is your favorite? Why?

VOCABULARY REVIEW

Word Chart

Copy this chart. Look at your Vocabulary words. Write the words where they belong on the chart.

Words That Rhyme with *tie*	Words About Time	Words About Books
fly		

LANGUAGE STRUCTURE REVIEW

Make Comparisons

Look at the pictures. How are they alike? How are they different? Talk about them with a partner. Answer these questions.

- Which rainbow is bigger?

- Which picture has brighter colors?

- Which picture do you like better? Why?

The PAPER

ICE CREAM

ICE CREAM

In My Community

My community is where I like to live!

My community is where I like to live!

I live and work and play

In my community every day.

My community is where I like to live!

Sing to the tune of
"If You're Happy and You Know It, Clap Your Hands."

259

Main Idea

Look at the picture below. Think about what the picture is mostly about. Then read this sentence.

The kittens are playing.

This sentence tells the main idea of the picture.

Try This

▶ Look at these pictures and read the sentences. Which sentence tells the main idea?

- **The fence is small.**
- **The boys are at the playground.**

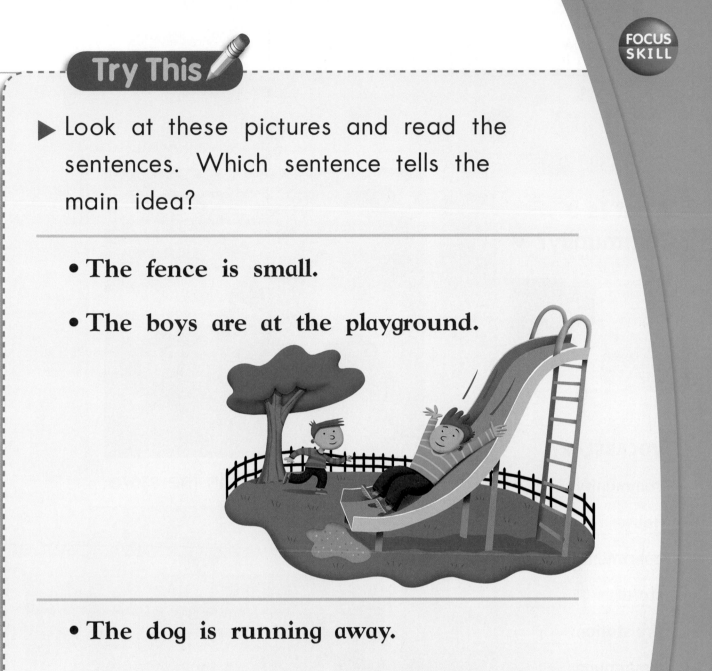

- **The dog is running away.**
- **The house is made of bricks.**

Vocabulary POWER

What Is a Community? ▼

VOCABULARY

community

house

apartment building

store

fire station

playground

She will buy apples in the **store**.

We like to play on the **playground**.

One family can live in a **house**.

Many families can live in an **apartment building**.

The fire truck is at the **fire station**.

There is a parade in the **community**.

What Is a Community?

A **community** is where people live, work, and play. Each community has places that make it special.

house

apartment building

Some people live in a house.
Some people live in an
apartment building. Where
else can people live?

Some people work in a store.
Some people work in a fire station.
Where else can people work?

store

fire station

FIRE STATION NO. 1

playground

Some people play at a playground.
Where else can people play?

Places in a Community

post office

school

library

bank

MONTCLAIR SAVINGS BANK

CARNEGIE PUBLIC LIBRARY

Think Critically

1 What is a community?

2 What is the main idea of this selection?

3 Where do people live, work, and play in your community?

4 What is your favorite place in your community?

Vocabulary POWER

Shoe Town ▼

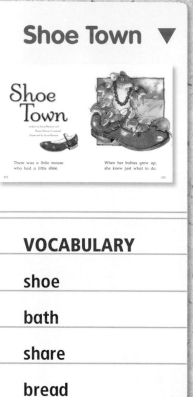

VOCABULARY

shoe

bath

share

bread

town

Put one **shoe** on each foot.

Everyone will have some if we **share**.

I use **bread** to make a sandwich.

The girls are giving the dog a **bath**.

A **town** has houses and shops.

Shoe Town

written by Janet Stevens and
Susan Stevens Crummel
illustrated by Janet Stevens

There was a little mouse
who had a little shoe.

When her babies grew up,
she knew just what to do.

"I'll fill a hot bath.
Then I'll take a long nap."

Just then at her shoe
came a rap-tap-tap-tap.

"We are Tortoise and Hare.
We just went for a run.

Can we stay here with you
in your shoe? Oh, what fun!"

"My shoe is too little
for so many to share.

"Hey-diddle-diddle-dee. Now there are three!"

Look for a shoe if you please.
It can go over there."

"Now I'll fill a hot bath.
Then I'll take a long nap."

Just then at her shoe
came a rap-tap-tap-tap.

"I'm the Little Red Hen.
And I love making bread.

Is there room in your shoe
for one more?" she said.

"My shoe is too little
for so many to share.

"Hey-diddle-diddle-door. Now there are four!"

Look for a shoe if you please.
It can go over there."

More and more friends came.
The little town grew.
And to think it began
with a mouse and her shoe!

"Hey-diddle-diddle-doo! Hang on to your shoe!"

Think Critically

① What keeps happening again and again in the story?

② Why doesn't the mouse want to share her shoe?

③ Why do you think the title of this story is "Shoe Town"?

④ Which was your favorite animal in the story? Why?

Vocabulary POWER

Lions ▼

VOCABULARY

wild

female

lion

cubs

dinner

male

The **lion** is a **wild** animal.

A **female** person is a woman or a girl.

Baby bears are called **cubs**.

A **male** person is a man or a boy.

This family likes to eat **dinner** together.

Lions

female lion

Lions are wild cousins of house cats. This is a female lion and her young cubs. How many cubs do you see?

lion cub

Most wild cats live alone. Lions are different. Lions live in groups called prides. This pride of lions is out hunting for dinner.

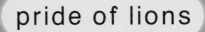

pride of lions

This **male** lion is doing what lions do a lot. He is taking a nap.

male lion

Animal Communities

zebras

monkeys

giraffes

hippos

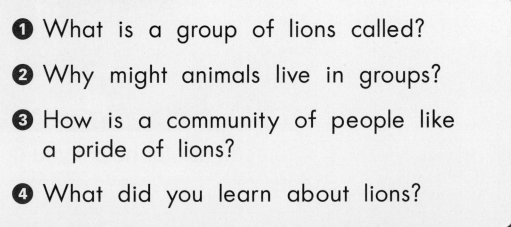

elephants

Think Critically

1. What is a group of lions called?

2. Why might animals live in groups?

3. How is a community of people like a pride of lions?

4. What did you learn about lions?

Vocabulary POWER

Did You See Chip? ▼

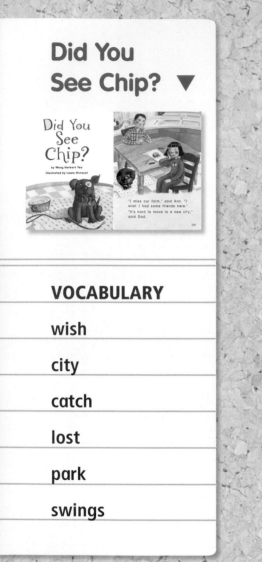

VOCABULARY

wish

city

catch

lost

park

swings

A big **city** has tall buildings.

You can ask for help if you are **lost**.

I **wish** I had a bone.

The boy wants to **catch** his friends.

A **park** has tall trees and green grass.

She likes to play on the **swings**.

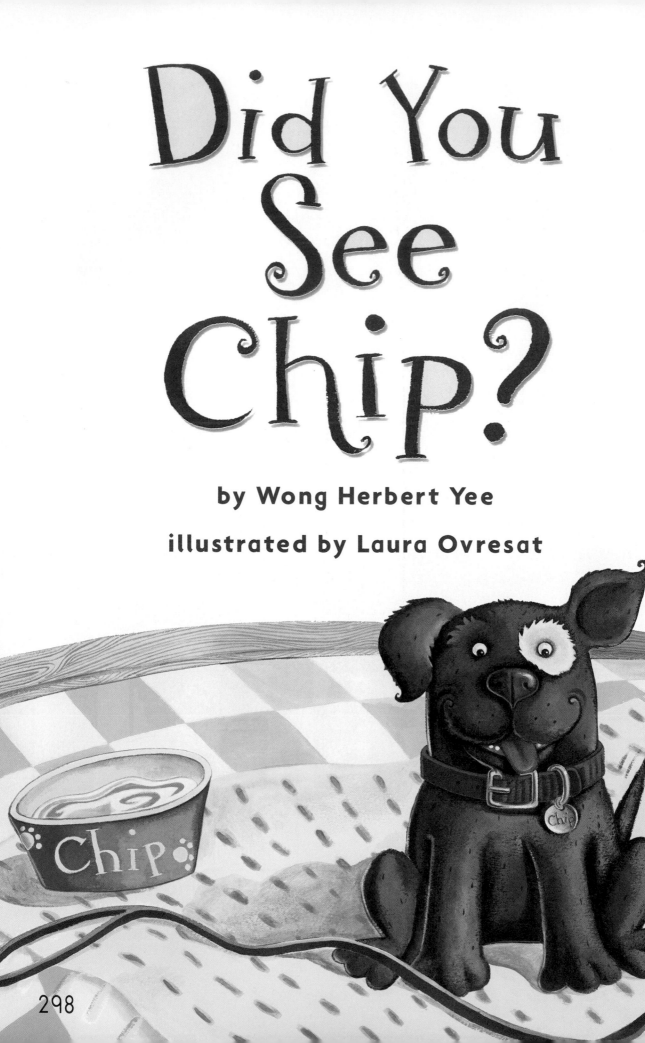

Did You See Chip?

by Wong Herbert Yee

illustrated by Laura Ovresat

"I miss our farm," said Ann. "I wish I had some friends here."

"It's hard to move to a new city," said Dad.

"Let's take Chip for a walk," said Dad. "That will help us cheer up."

"Chip!" yelled Ann. "Come back!"
"We have to catch him!" said Dad.
"He could get lost in this big city."

"Hi!" said Ann. "Did you see my dog, Chip?"

"Is he a little black dog?" asked Mr. Todd.

"Yes," said Dad.

"I think he ran to the park," said
Mr. Todd. "I'll help you catch him!"

"Hi!" said Ann. "Did you see
my dog, Chip?"

"Is he a little black dog?"
asked Mr. Ross.

"Yes," said Dad.

"I think he ran to the swings," said Mr. Ross. "I'll help you catch him!"

"Hi!" said Ann. "Did you see
my dog, Chip?"

"Is he a little black dog?"
asked Mrs. Mills.

"Yes," said Dad.

"I think he ran out of the park," said Mrs. Mills. "I'll help you catch him!"

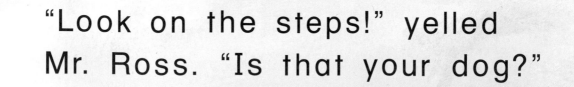

"Look on the steps!" yelled
Mr. Ross. "Is that your dog?"

"Yes, it's Chip!" said Ann. "Thanks!"

"Now we have new friends," said Dad, "and Chip helped us find them!"

Think Critically

1. Why do Ann and Dad rush out of their house?

2. How do Ann and Dad make new friends?

3. Do you think Ann will like the city more from now on? Why?

4. How would you feel if your pet ran away?

Review Vocabulary with a Play

STORIES ON STAGE

Review

VOCABULARY

town

store

lion

park

We've Come to Town

Characters

Children

Fran Field

Sam Store

Zina Zoo

Ron River

Pedro Park

311

Children: We've come to town. Hurray!
Where should we go first today?

Sam Store: Come and see my new toys.
And my games for girls
and boys!

Ron River: Come see me. Ride on a boat. You can also swim and float.

Fran Field: Come see me. You'll have fun. Come play ball in the sun!

313

Zina Zoo: Come and see a lion roar,
Apes, birds, and so much more!

Children: There's so much to see and do!
Should we see the store or zoo?

Pedro Park: Come see me. Sit by a tree. You can plan what you will see.

Children: That is what we will do. Thanks, Park! We'll go see YOU!

315

Review Activities

Think and Respond

1 How are the stories alike?

2 How do the animals in "Shoe Town" make a community?

3 Which community would you like to visit? Why?

4 How do the people help Ann in "Did You See Chip?"

5 Which stories helped you learn something? What did you learn?

VOCABULARY REVIEW

Word Webs

Make word webs with your Vocabulary words. Group words that belong together. Add more words that you know.

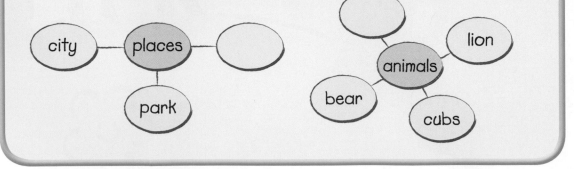

Give Commands

Look at the picture. Read the command that Ann said to Chip. Did Chip do what Ann said? Now look through the play, "We've Come to Town." Find the commands these characters say.

- Sam Store
- Fran Field
- Zina Zoo
- Pedro Park
- Ron River

Chip! Come back!

SING ALONG

Great Big World

All around this great big world,

Great big world,

Great big world,

All around this great big world

We will travel!

Sing to the tune of
"London Bridge Is Falling Down."

Using Picture Clues

Do you know what the word <u>astronaut</u> means? Read the sentence below. Then look at the picture. The picture will give you clues about what <u>astronaut</u> means.

The astronaut is going on a trip.

The picture shows a rocket and a person in a space suit. These clues tell you that an astronaut is a person who explores space.

Try This

▶ Read each sentence. Then look at the pictures. Use the pictures to help you understand new words.

We sailed to the <u>island</u>.

What is an <u>island</u>? How did the picture help you?

The children <u>leaped</u> over the box.

What does <u>leaped</u> mean? How did the picture help you?

Vocabulary POWER

Our Family Comes from 'Round the World ▼

VOCABULARY

world

happy

big

young

old

short

tall

A globe helps us learn about the **world**.

The **happy** children give a cheer.

322

The **young** goat walks on the hay.

Some buildings are very **old**.

The girl looks **short** next to her **big** dog.

Giraffes are **tall** animals.

Our Family
Comes from
'Round
the
World

by Mary Ann Hoberman

Our family comes
From 'round the world:
Our hair is straight,
Our hair is curled,
Our eyes are brown,
Our eyes are blue,
Our skins are different
Colors, too.

Tra la tra la
Tra la tra lee
We're one big happy family!

We're girls and boys,
We're big and small,
We're young and old,
We're short and tall.
We're everything
That we can be
And still we are
A family.

O la dee da
O la dee dee
We're one big happy family!

We laugh and cry,
We work and play,
We help each other
Every day.
The world's a lovely
Place to be
Because we are
A family.

Hurray hurrah
Hurrah hurree
We're one big happy family!

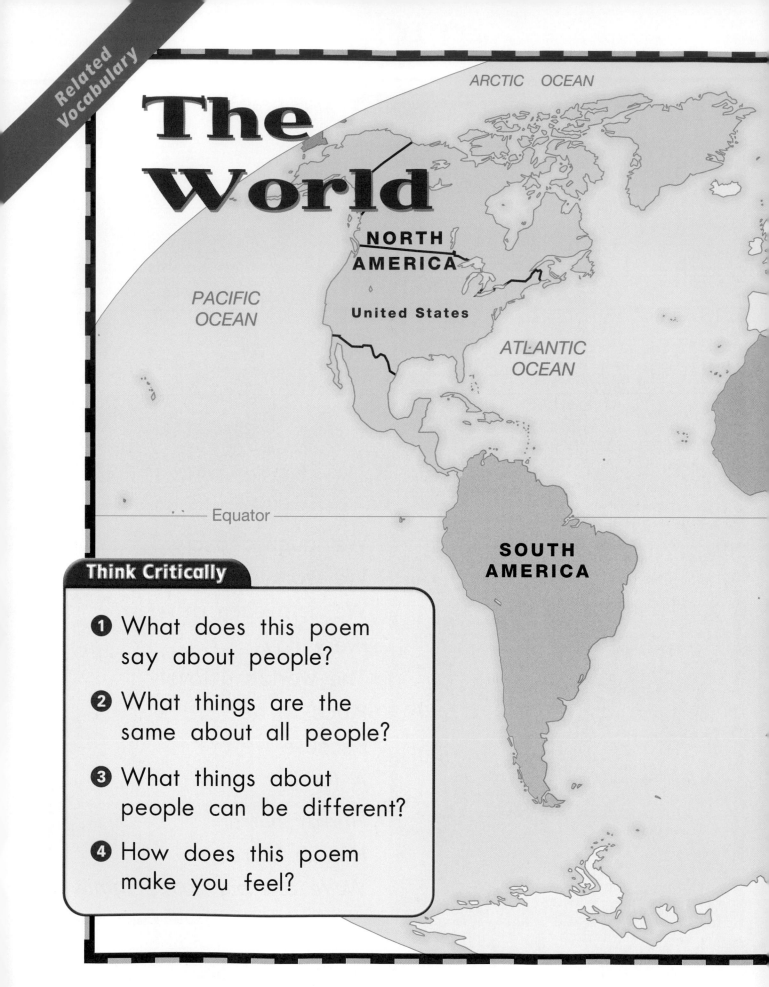

ARCTIC OCEAN

The World

NORTH AMERICA

United States

PACIFIC OCEAN

ATLANTIC OCEAN

Equator

SOUTH AMERICA

Think Critically

❶ What does this poem say about people?

❷ What things are the same about all people?

❸ What things about people can be different?

❹ How does this poem make you feel?

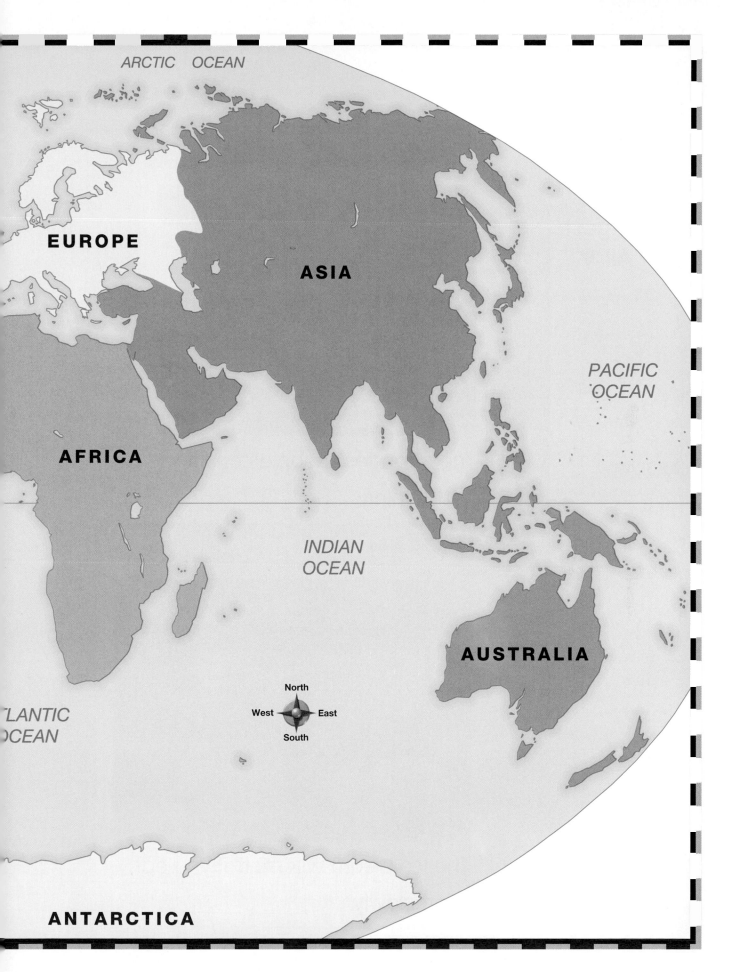

ARCTIC OCEAN

EUROPE

ASIA

PACIFIC OCEAN

AFRICA

INDIAN OCEAN

AUSTRALIA

ATLANTIC OCEAN

North
West — East
South

ANTARCTICA

329

Vocabulary POWER

The Strongest One of All ▼

VOCABULARY

strongest

melt

earth

push

The **strongest** people can lift heavy things.

The ice cream will **melt** if you eat it too slowly.

She will **push** the baby in the stroller.

The roots push down into the **earth**.

The Strongest One of All

retold by Mirra Ginsburg

illustrated by

Jose Aruego & Ariane Dewey

A lamb slipped on the ice and cried, "Ice, ice, you made me fall. Are you strong? Are you the strongest one of all?"

The ice answered, "If I were the strongest, would the sun melt me?"

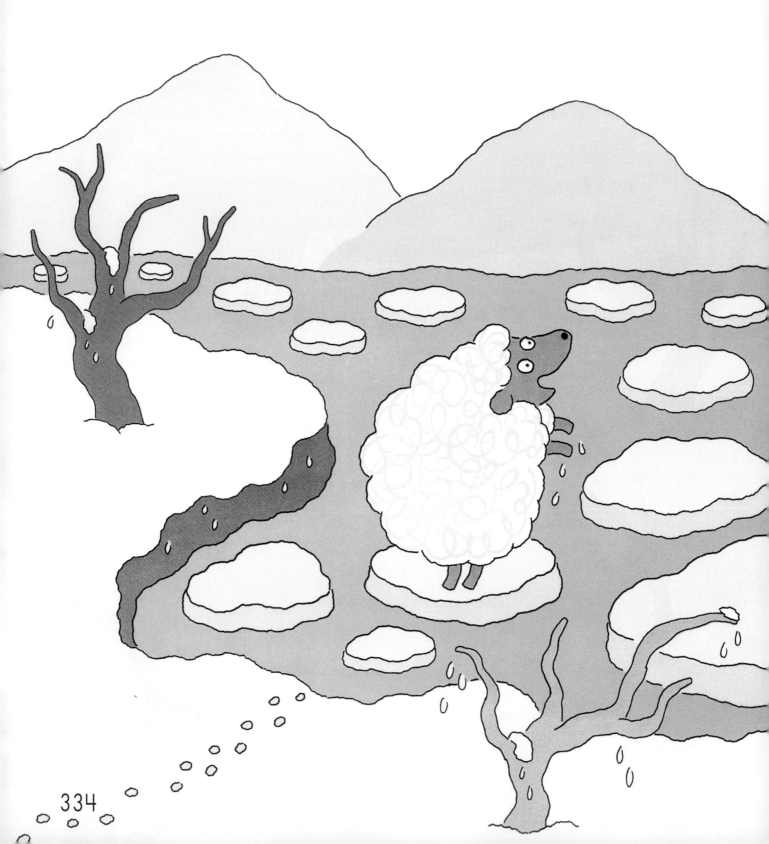

The lamb went to the sun and asked, "Sun, sun, are you the strongest one of all?"

The sun answered, "If I were the strongest, would the cloud cover me?"

The lamb went to the cloud and asked, "Cloud, cloud, are you the strongest one of all?"

The cloud answered, "If I were the strongest, would I scatter into rain?"

The lamb went to the rain and asked, "Rain, rain, are you the strongest one of all?"

The rain answered, "If I were the strongest, would the earth swallow me?"

The lamb went to the earth
and asked, "Earth, earth, are
you the strongest one of all?"

The earth answered, "If I
were the strongest, would the
grass push its roots down
through me?"

341

340

The lamb went to the grass and asked, "Grass, grass, are you the strongest one of all?"

The grass answered, "If I were the strongest, would a lamb eat me?"

The lamb jumped with joy.
"I may slip, and I may fall,
but I'm the strongest! I'm
the strongest of them all!"

Think Critically

1 Who is the strongest one of all?

2 Why did the lamb think that the ice was the strongest?

3 What is the setting at the beginning? How does it change?

4 Did the ending of the story surprise you? Why or why not?

Vocabulary POWER

Man on the Moon ▼

MAN ON THE MOON
BY FRANKLIN M. BRANLEY

moon car

Twelve astronauts have gone to the moon. They walked on the moon. Some of these astronauts rode in a moon car.

astronaut

VOCABULARY

astronauts

moon

outside

rocks

mountains

hills

explore

We can see the **moon** tonight.

Astronauts wear space suits.

344

It's fun to **explore** **outside**.

Some **mountains** have snow on top.

There are many **rocks** by the water.

The sky over the **hills** is cloudy.

MAN ON THE MOON

BY FRANKLYN M. BRANLEY

astronaut

moon car

Twelve astronauts have gone to the moon. They walked on the moon. Some of these astronauts rode in a moon car.

The astronauts found no air on the moon. Outside their ship, the men wore space suits. The air they needed was carried inside the suits.

space suit

rock

They found small rocks and great
big ones. Some were as big as a house.

Parts of the moon are flat. In those places, the astronauts could move quite easily. There are many mountains and hills. Some are smooth and rounded. Some have large jagged rocks sticking out of them.

hills

There are cliffs and deep valleys.
The astronauts kept away from them.

Someday astronauts may go to the moon again. Once more they may explore it. They may put up buildings on the moon and live inside them. They may start a moon colony.

Who knows, someday you may work in a moon colony. You may be a moon explorer. Then you'll see for yourself what the moon is like.

SPACE TRAVEL

space shuttle

Earth

354

moon

space station

space suit

Think Critically

❶ What did the astronauts see on the moon?

❷ Why do you think astronauts stayed away from the cliffs and valleys?

❸ Why might people want to go to the moon again?

❹ Where would you like to go if you were an astronaut?

Vocabulary POWER

Tell Me a Story ▼

VOCABULARY

cook

dreams

river

boats

island

sail

sea

scared

I like to **cook** with my sister and my dad.

They were alone on the **river**.

They use the wind to **sail** their **boats**.

The boy cried because he was **scared**.

I am an artist in my **dreams**.

The **sea** is all around the **island**.

357

Tell Me a Story

by Alma Flor Ada

illustrated by Gerardo Suzán

"Tell me a story, Abuelita," said Camila. "Tell me a story about long ago."

"What would you like to hear? Would you like to hear about your father when he was a young man?"

"No, Abuelita. Tell me about when you were a little girl."

"Listen, Camila, and I will tell you. When I was a little girl, my family did not own a car. We didn't ride places. We walked."

"That must have been hard, Abuelita. Did you stop to rest a lot?"

"It was fine, Camila. Walking is fun."

"Tell me more, Abuelita."

"We didn't have many of the things we have today. We had to use coal to cook."

"Did you cook with coal every day?"

"Of course we did, Camila. We had
to cook every day, and we always
used coal."

"My friends and I had such fun! We played outside in front of the house. We liked to jump rope on the sidewalk."

"Why did you play in front of the house, Abuelita?"

"We played there because it was the best place to play, Camila."

"What did you like most when you were young, Abuelita?"

"I liked flying kites. On windy days, the kites went very far up. I let my dreams fly with the kites."

"I can imagine all the kites,
Abuelita! I would like my
dreams to fly high, too!"

"Oh, but my favorite place was the river."

"The river? Why did you like the river, Abuelita?"

"There was a big tree at the side of the river. I would sit on a branch and look down. I could see ducks, fish, and bullfrogs."

"Bullfrogs? Didn't they scare you,
Abuelita?"

"Oh, no, Camila. It was fun. I
had the best time at the river."

"I made boats and sent them
down the river. I would picture
them landing on a beautiful
island. I wished I could sail
with them. I wished I could sail
all the way to the sea."

"I would sail with you! I would
go all the way to the sea. I
wouldn't be scared, Abuelita!"

"One day, we will sail together
to the sea. We will, Camila!"

1 Who is Abuelita?

2 What does Abuelita share with Camila?

3 For each story Abuelita shares, there are two pictures. How are those two pictures different?

4 Which of Abuelita's stories do you like best? Why?

Review Vocabulary with a Play

★ STORIES ON STAGE ★

In Our Dreams

Review

VOCABULARY

dreams

explore

moon

earth

strongest

big

sail

tall

Characters

Rosa

Stan

David

Marvin

Lily

Felix

Friends

Friends: Rosa, what are your dreams?

Rosa: In my dreams, I explore the moon! I can see the earth from space!

Felix: Me, too!

Friends: David, what are your dreams?

David: In my dreams, I am the strongest! I can lift big rocks!

Felix: Me, too!

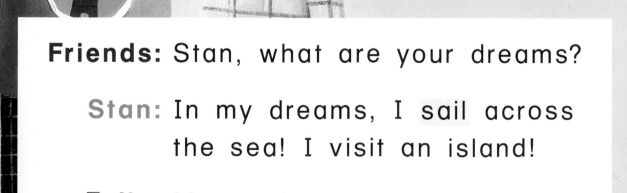

Friends: Stan, what are your dreams?

Stan: In my dreams, I sail across the sea! I visit an island!

Felix: Me, too!

Friends: Marvin, what are your dreams?

Marvin: In my dreams, I climb a tall
mountain! I put a flag on top.

Felix: Me, too!

Friends: Lily, what are your dreams?

Lily: In my dreams, I paddle my boat down a river! It's a fast ride!

Felix: Not me!

Friends: Why not, Felix?

Felix: I have my own dreams. I'm hungry, and I'm dreaming of a nice big sandwich.

Friends: Oh, Felix!

Review Activities

Think and Respond

1. Which characters explore things? What do they explore?

2. How is "Man on the Moon" different from the other selections in Unit 6?

3. The lamb and the astronauts learned many new things. What did they learn?

4. Which places would you like to visit? Why?

5. How are all the stories alike?

VOCABULARY REVIEW

Make a Word Square

Write a Vocabulary word and draw a picture for it. Write sentences with the word.

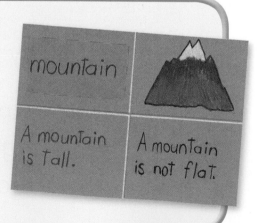

mountain

A mountain is tall.

A mountain is not flat.

Describe Routines

Draw three boxes. Write three things you do every morning at school. Share your chart with a partner and tell about it.

First, we say the pledge.

Next, we change the calendar.

Last, we sing a song.

Glossary

What Is a Glossary?

A glossary is like a small dictionary. You can use it when you need to know what a word means. You can look up the word and read it in a sentence. Some words have a picture to help you.

bird   That **bird** has colorful feathers.

A

ants   The **ants** crawled on the ground.

a·part·ment build·ing   We live in a tall **apartment building**.

ap·ples   We picked **apples** from a tree.

arms   I use my **arms** to hug my friend.

ar·tist   The **artist** is painting a picture.

as·tro·nauts   The **astronauts** travel into space.

B

ba·nan·as   The monkey ate **bananas**.

base·ball   The **baseball** player hit the ball with a bat.

bea·vers   **Beavers** use wood to build their homes.

bird   That **bird** has colorful feathers.

apples

artist

baseball

bird

books

chick

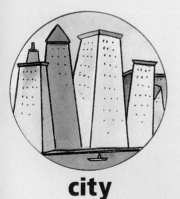

city

boats   The **boats** sail on the water.

books   I read some **books** about dinosaurs.

born   My baby sister was **born** at the hospital.

C

catch   When you throw the ball, I will **catch** it.

chick   A **chick** hatches from an egg.

chin   A long beard grew from his **chin**.

cit•y   The **city** has many tall buildings.

class   I have many friends in my **class**.

cook   I help my father **cook** dinner.

crops   The farmer grows **crops** of corn, wheat, and beans.

cubs   Young bear **cubs** like to play.

D

dog   The **dog** barked.

down   The ball bounced up and **down**.

E

eat   I **eat** dinner with my family.

eggs   The hen sits on her **eggs**.

ex•plore   Astronauts **explore** space.

eyes   The cat's **eyes** are yellow.

F

fall   **Fall** is the season that comes before winter.

fam•i•lies   Many **families** live in our neighborhood.

farm   Cows, horses, and pigs live on a **farm**.

dog

fall

farm

flowers

grapes

happy

fe·male   **Female** lions care for lion cubs.

fire sta·tion   Firefighters work at a
   fire station.

flow·ers   Ana picked **flowers** from the
   garden.

fly   Birds **fly** through the air.

fruit   Bananas and grapes are **fruit**.

G

good-bye   I say **good-bye** to my friends
   when I leave school.

grapes   I ate some **grapes** with my lunch.

H

hands   We raise our **hands** to ask questions.

hap·py   I smile when I am **happy**.

390

hel•lo   My neighbor says **hello** to me every day.

help   Tara needs **help** to tie her shoes.

hens   The **hens** lay eggs.

high   The plane flies **high** in the air.

hip•po   A **hippo** is a very large animal.

house   I live in a yellow **house**.

hippo

K

kick   How far can you **kick** the ball?

knees   Tim scraped both of his **knees**.

kick

L

learn   We **learn** many things at school.

leaves   Most plants have green **leaves**.

leaves

lion

melt

moon

li·brar·y   I read books at the **library**.

like   I **like** to draw pictures.

li·on   The **lion** roars loudly.

lis·ten   **Listen** to the music.

lost   I **lost** my jacket and cannot find it.

M

makes   He **makes** salad for dinner.

male   My father and brother are **male**.

man   A boy grows up to be a **man**.

melt   This ice will **melt** in the sun.

mix   We **mix** flour and milk for pancakes.

moon   I can see the **moon** in the night sky.

N

nap   The babies **nap** each day.

nose   When I have a cold, I blow my **nose**.

O

old   The **old** car does not work.

P

paint   We like to **paint** pictures.

park   I walk my dog in the **park**.

pet   Our class **pet** is a rabbit.

plant   The **plant** grows because we water it every day.

play   I **play** games with my sister.

play•ground   I like the swings at the **playground**.

nap

old

pet

river

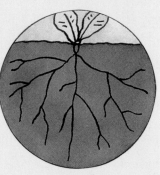

roots

salad

plums   The **plums** taste sweet.

pre•tend   We will **pretend** to be wild animals.

push   I **push** the cart at the market.

R

read   I **read** funny stories.

ride   Jim and Bob **ride** their bikes to school.

riv•er   Boats sail down the **river**.

rocks   Some **rocks** are next to the tree.

roots   The plant's **roots** grow under the ground.

rules   We follow the **rules** at school.

S

sail   The girls **sail** their boat in the pond.

sal•ad   I put mushrooms in the **salad**.

scared   Sometimes I am **scared** when it is dark.

school   I ride the bus to **school**.

seeds   We planted **seeds** in the garden.

share   I **share** my toys with my friends.

shoe   This **shoe** goes on the left foot.

small   A squirrel is a **small** animal.

smiled   I **smiled** because I was happy.

soc•cer   My brother plays on a **soccer** team.

spring   The weather is warm in **spring**.

store   We buy food at the **store**.

stor•ies   This book has many **stories**.

school

shoe

small

soccer

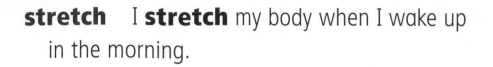

sun

swim

teacher

stretch   I **stretch** my body when I wake up in the morning.

sun   The **sun** is warm and bright.

sur•prise   My sister's birthday party was a **surprise**.

swim   I **swim** at the pool.

T

talk   I **talk** to my cousins on the telephone.

teach•er   My **teacher** helps me learn.

team   Ricky's **team** won the game.

toes   I can touch my **toes** when I bend over.

to•geth•er   We walk to school **together**.

tools   My father uses **tools** to fix things.

town   A **town** is smaller than a city.

try   **Try** to catch the ball.

U

use   I **use** a towel to dry my hands.

W

wall   She put a poster on the **wall**.

win   We want to **win** the game.

win•ter   **Winter** is very cold.

world   The **world** has many countries.

Y

young   The kitten is **young**.

town

winter

young

Acknowledgments

For permission to reprint copyrighted material, grateful acknowledgment is made to the following sources:

HarperCollins Publishers: From *What the Moon Is Like* (Retitled: "Man on the Moon") by Franklyn M. Branley. Text copyright © 1963, 1986 by Franklyn M. Branley. "The Strongest One of All" from *Merry-Go-Round: Four Stories* by Mirra Ginsburg, illustrated by Jose Aruego and Ariane Dewey. Text copyright © 1969, 1973, 1977, 1981 by Mirra Ginsburg; illustrations copyright © 1977, 1981, 1992 by Jose Aruego and Ariane Dewey.

Little, Brown and Company (Inc.): "Our Family Comes from 'Round the World" from *Fathers, Mothers, Sisters, Brothers* by Mary Ann Hoberman. Text copyright © 1991 by Mary Ann Hoberman.

The McGraw-Hill Companies: "Stretch, Stretch" from *Rhymes for Learning Times* by Louise Binder Scott. Text copyright © 1983 by T. S. Denison & Co., Inc.

Scholastic Inc.: "Good-by and Hello" (Retitled: "Good-bye and Hello") by Barbara Anthony from *Poetry Place Anthology.* Text copyright © 1983 by Edgell Communications, Inc. From *Seeds Grow!* by Angela Shelf Medearis, illustrated by Jill Dubin. Text copyright © 1999 by Angela Shelf Medearis; illustrations copyright © 1999 by Jill Dubin. A *Hello Reader!* Book. Published by Cartwheel Books, a division of Scholastic Inc.

Viking Children's Books, a member of Penguin Group (USA) Inc.: When the TV Broke by Harriet Ziefert, illustrated by Mavis Smith. Text copyright © 1989 by Harriet Ziefert; illustrations copyright © 1989 by Mavis Smith.

Photo Credits

Page Placement Key: (t)-top (c)-center (b)-bottom (l)-left (r)-right (fg)-foreground (bg)-background.

18 Mark E. Gibson;19-29 Harcourt; 30 Bill Bachmann/Alamy Images; 31 Harcourt; 32 Larry Dale Gordon/Getty Images; 33 Jose L. Pelaez/Corbis Stock Market; 34-35 Bill Bachmann/Alamy Images;36-45 Harcourt; 46 (t) Jose Luis Pelaez/Corbis; 46 (b) Harcourt; 47 (t) International Stock/Image State; 47 (b) Harcourt; 71 Harcourt; 76 Harcourt; 77 (t) David Woods/Corbis; 77 (b) Harcourt; 86-95 Harcourt; 96 (t) Anthony Bannister; Gallo Images/Corbis; 96 Harcourt; 97 (t),(tl), (tr) Harcourt; 97 b) Eisenhut & Mayer/FoodPix; 97 (bl) & (br) Harcourt; 98 Gay Bumgarner/Getty Images; 99 Victoria McCormick/Animals Animals/Earth Scenes; 100 Carol Hughes/Bruce Coleman, Inc.; 101 Terry E. Eiler/Stock, Boston; 102 (b) Harcourt; 103 (tl), (tr),& (bl) Harcourt; 103 (br) Peter Adams/ImageState; 128-140 Harcourt; 141 (t) Harcourt; 141 (b) Corbis; 152-153 Harcourt; 154-155 Tom Stewart/Corbis Stock Market; 156-157 Mark E. Gibson; 158 (inset) Harcourt; 158 Jim Cummins/Getty Images; 159 (b) William Manning/Corbis Stock Market; 159 (tl) C. Lee/Getty Images; 159 (tr) Steve Dunwell/Getty Images; 160 (t) Harcourt; 160 (b) Michael Pole/Corbis; 161-191 Harcourt; 198-226 Harcourt; 227 (t) Harcourt; 227 (bl) Michael Newman/PhotoEdit; 227 (br) Harcourt; 228 Harcourt; 229 (t) Stephen Frisch/Stock, Boston; 229 (c) & (b) Harcourt; 230 (l) & (r) Harcourt; 230 (c) Jeff Greenberg/Photo Researchers; 231 (t) Inge Morath/Magnum Photos; 231 (c)& (b) Harcourt; 232 (t) Harcourt; 232 (b) Bachmann/Stock, Boston; 233-249 Harcourt; 262 Harcourt; 263 (tl) & (tr) Harcourt; 263 (bl) Kevin Fleming/Corbis; 263 (br) Ariel Skelley/Corbis; 264 Joseph Sohm/Visions of America, LLC/PictureQuest; 265 (r) Debra Cohn-Orbach/Index Stock Imagery; 265 (inset) Corbis Stock Market; 266-267 Harcourt; 268 (t) Mark C. Burnett/Stock, Boston; 268 (c) Bill Horsman/Stock, Boston; 268-269 (b) Michael S. Yamashita/Corbis; 269 (t) Mark C. Burnett/Photo Researchers; 269 (c) John Lei/Stock, Boston; 270-289 Harcourt; 290-291 Klaus-Peter Wolf/Animals Animals/Earth Scenes; 292 Bill Ruth/Bruce Coleman, Inc.; 293 John Chellman/Animals Animals/Earth Scenes; 294 (t) Art Wolfe/Photo Researchers; 294 (c) Ernest A. Janes/Bruce Coleman, Inc.; 294 (b) Rick Edwards/Animals Animals/Earth Scenes; 295 (t) Bruce Davidson/Animals Animals/Earth Scenes; 295 (b) Art Wolfe/Photo Researchers; 296-297 Harcourt; 310-323 Harcourt; 324 (l) Lawrence Migdale; 324 (r) Ariel Skelley/Corbis; 325 (l) Ariel Skelley/Corbis; 325 (r) Wartenberg/Picture Press/Corbis; 326 (t) The Photographers' Library/Uniphoto; 326 (bl) Paul Barton/Corbis Stock Market; 326 (br) Paul Barton/Corbis Stock Market; 327 (b) Ariel Skelley/Corbis Stock Market; 327 (tl) Lawrence Migdale; 327 (tr) Robert Brenner/PhotoEdit; 330 (t) Harcourt; 330 (b) Royalty-Free/Corbis; 331 (t) Royalty-Free/Corbis; 331 (b) Grant Heilman Photograpy; 344 Harcourt; 345 (tl),(tr),& (bl) Harcourt; 345 (br) Royalty-Free/Corbis; 346-355 NASA; 356-357 Harcourt; Page 387 (both), 388, 389 (both), 390 (both), , 391 (t), 391 (b), 392, Harcourt Telescope; 393, Harcourt Index; 394, Harcourt Telescope; 395 (t), David Preston; 395 (b), Harcourt Telescope; 396 (t), Harcourt Telescope 396 (c), (b), Harcourt Index; 397, Harcourt Telescope.

Illustration Credits

Steve Johnson and Lou Fancher, 14-15; Winky Adam, 16-17; Laura Ovresat, 62-71, 298-309; Rosario Valderrama, 74-75; Lisa Campbell Ernst, 78-87, 250-257; Jose Aruego and Ariane Dewey, 104-113, 332-343; Mircea Catusanu, 114-123; Laurence Cleyet-Merle, 124-125; Donna Ingemanson, 126-127; Brian Karas, 142-151; Jill Dubin, 162-175; Julie Carpenter, 176-185, 316-317; Gary Taxali, 186-187; Dona Turner, 188-189; Tracy Sabin, 192-197; Mavis Smith, 200-225; Ed Martinez, 236-249; Mircea Catusanu, 258-259; Benoit Laverdiere, 318-319; June Michel, 320-321; Leah Palmer Preiss, 324-327; Bob Depew, 352-353; Gerardo Suzan, 358-375; Emilie Chollat, 376-385; Jennifer Herbert, 387-397.